EXPLODING

FIRST POETS SERIES 6

SERIES EDITOR: ELANA WOLFF

**Canada Council
for the Arts**

**Conseil des Arts
du Canada**

Guernica Editions Inc. acknowledges the support of
the Canada Council for the Arts.

SANDY POOL

EXPLODING
INTO NIGHT

GUERNICA
TORONTO – BUFFALO – CHICAGO – LANCASTER (U.K.)
2009

Elana Wolff, editor
Guernica Editions Inc.
P.O. Box 117, Station P, Toronto (ON), Canada M5S 2S6
2250 Military Road, Tonawanda, N.Y. 14150-6000 U.S.A.

Distributors:
University of Toronto Press Distribution,
5201 Dufferin Street, Toronto (ON), Canada M3H 5T8
Gazelle Book Services, White Cross Mills, High Town,
Lancaster LA1 4XS U.K.
Independent Publishers Group,
814 N. Franklin Street, Chicago, Il. 60610 U.S.A.

First edition.
Printed in Canada.

Legal Deposit – Fourth Quarter
Library of Congress Catalog Card Number: 2009936987
Library and Archives Canada Cataloguing in Publication
Pool, Sandy
Exploding into night / Sandy Pool. — 1st ed.
(First poets series ; 6)
Poems.
ISBN 978-1-55071-307-7
I. Title. II. Series: First poets series (Toronto, Ont.) ; 6
PS8631.O622E96 2009   C811'.6   C2009-905709-3

For Parkdale, and for Rose

I promised to show you a map you say but this is
        a mural
then yes let it be   these are small distinctions
where do we see it from is the question

                                        Adrienne Rich,
                            An Atlas of the Difficult World

Here is her street at dusk. The slick sheen of streetlamps glowing over Parkdale. Here is her street, open mouthed, desolate. Tulips long dead, no traffic. Even the park closed down. Panic of needles, small wasps crouching in sand. On Landsdowne, Sunday bells flood out from the little Portuguese church where Nathan still works the corner. Survivors scavenge the shoreline, looking for fuselage.

It isn't supposed to end like this, blood burdening the lake. Spring and the scientists baffled. Nuclear run-off, all the carp dead. At night her street is silent, the stench of fish over Parkdale. You swear you don't smell it; love, the sudden absence.

Look closer. The houses backlit. Streetlamps burning their filaments. It is here you tell me about history, foundations constructed without the convenience of machines.

When we reach the boardwalk, the lake lashes us, its giant tongue pointing towards the power plant. Horizon folding into dark. We open a cheap bottle of wine, make love on the beach as if we know someone is watching.

At night the Vanduras come alive. They lurk, quiet as jaguars down Roncesvalles in their milk-white cabs, searching for anything that moves. Cats are disappearing by the dozen, hydro poles teeming with faded portraits of toddlers and their pets. Soon there will be others. Lured into hell-mouthed double doors, sped off to some inconspicuous location.

Every Sunday my mother calls to tell me about some kid who's gone missing in this city. I'm not surprised. I don't tell her about the cats, or those white vans, disembodied specters roaring into dark.

Underwater city – fluid tongues flickering in moonlight. Electricity ignites our palms, burns a kiss in our mouths. We sway with the streetcar tracks. Warm and wet, your deaf heart holds two mirrors exacting shape. I lean you against the newly painted wall, leave the faint impression of backbone. This quick embrace – apogamy. Algae blooming in dark water.

You pin me against the wall, where the fat moths beat themselves senseless. Mantis mouthed, I lean in, hungry for salt, saliva. The porch lights burn for hours. You have been waiting to take me here, body splayed out, limbs akimbo. The light runs ragged across my face. Neighbours turn on their lights, "you fucking sonofabitch," but you keep going. We both know you will never touch me like this again.

Do not say anything. Tongue pressed against my neck. Bones of history, still brittle in our mouths. This is the broken timbre of your voice. Silence, the incessant dirge, drowning you out. City smeared against a white scrap of sky. Your body aching. Here you slept, all sweat and salt, where the sheets pulled from the mattress.

It's spring. The sparrow dies instantly. Quick bang, the streetcar suspended. Small black body. You can still see the white speckled across its back, small grains of rice; twittering youth. You insist on a proper burial. Together we glide through the city, bird cupped in your palm. The concrete, post-rain, bleak and lunar.

We speak elliptically, sleep-talk about death. Wings immobilized in flight. The air thickens as we breathe out. Our hulls contain us, solemn as prayer, delicate shells of bone.

It is enough to undo this desire. Unhinged, it becomes something else – light jammed under a door, a piece of jade. At night you hear the creaking pine, the kerosene hiss. It tells you nothing. Siren song lapping against shore, flickering with the opalescent moon. Your body – sinuous shadow against the wall.

Your body moves through water, elegant grotesque – a water beetle without sound. When you finally speak, voice echoes across the lake, cuts through the rain, the haunted crying of loons.

In time, our cottage eludes us – dissolves into squares of lemon coloured light. We swim, limbs surface and resurface. We shuck ourselves nightly, unholy skins, driftwood bones. In the dark we write psalms to the awkward silence. Loneliness, that solemn habit, gaining.

The light measures itself against the contours of your beautiful legs. Curls an arm around you as you sleep. I can hardly bear it – sunlight precarious, sperm and must in my hair. Tonight I sleep so far from you, dreaming of ocean. Jellyfish heart bloating, raw and iridescent. I remember something about velocity and fear – elegant Houdini, a wrist slit, no warning.

We are mouthing the words. Famished tongues circling with the grace of a thousand lemon trees swaying in rain. We ordered Chinese food, discussed the future. I had tried to love you before and failed. You leaned me back, whispered, pushing yourself into me. "Take it, please." Kept running your skilled hands across my heart. "Take it." Bodies hard-pressed with humidity, peonies unfurling in rain.

Dull scrape in the stomach – lovesick pigeons mewling in the laneway. Bowl of grapes, decrepit on the windowsill. Your head bent, listening for something. You can't hear it – silence sweeping the concrete, cutting hard lines against your face. Consider this failure: a kiss on any street corner, hopeful as morning.

Mosquitoes flood the cracks, ravage our bodies. We make love. The tamarack smacks against the wall. Afterwards you apologize for the blood-let, rub calamine into my thigh, tell me how nice it is to be here. This love infested place.

This is not faith. Security of unseeing; blood infiltrating blood. My hand against the small of your back, pulse of metabolism. Skin pulled over us – threadbare. Survival not merely endurance, but also the act of knowing. One will help the other die.

The landfill of dream is frantic. Perverse tufts of fur and bone adorn your body. You lean over and whisper into my ear, "You'll never get out of this." True, and not true. Coming back that night was a mistake.

The women were already crowding. They, too, touched by your eloquence, your inevitable dead-ends.

In sleep I offer my organs. Pink, pulsing and wild. It's not enough, but all I can muster. If I could, I'd offer you sea-light; the milk white skin of my eye.

Shock is present in varying degrees. If you are hurt badly, I don't notice. I stare hard at the morning paper. There is nothing I can do. Your flesh is so different from my own. In the fragile incision of silence, small cuts keep us safe.

You came from nowhere, arbitrary crocus rising from snow. I was uncomfortable in your presence. Candy underwear, liquid fructose dribbling down my legs. I awoke hung over, small and anxious against your frame.

In a dream I'd made love to a bear and enjoyed it. Skin tearing open, blood-bright. That morning, we fought about something. It wasn't the lipstick on glass or even the weak sex. It was the dirty fingernails when you came home. I kept thinking there were bits of her stuck under them.

It became routine to love you, like rinsing out the teapot or feeding the cat. Sometimes I imagined you unzipping yourself for other lovers, popping open like a seed-pod, showing off your new growth. I imagined women preening with joy to see your delicate armour so exposed.

In the end you got what you wanted: dishware, the TV. I have what was between us; a blighted ovum.

I have forgotten how to speak. Silenced by the weight of things. Morse code into the receiver, "I love you, I love you." So what. Your heart keeps pumping, as if all it knows is circulation.

There's no room for sentiment here, the lines between us so thin and dark. No trick in the landscape either; if we set this in a pond, one of us would be Leda.

A white rush, sudden blow: static. We retreat to separate apartments. Conspiracies collecting like sediment. Every door shut seems slammed.

I never liked that suit. It stank of your father, held you deadly inside it. You threatened to kill me as I was lighting the crème brûlée. Something about the roast not being rare enough, or too rare. I don't remember now. I was tired of love and its subsidiaries. The way the roast dripped, or did not drip, blood on your plate.

When they ask, I say we are happy. Either one or both of us. Your eyes, two electric eels searching the dark. Questions I can't answer. You know the difference. That break in your voice. You know it is your insides dropping hollow and sharp into place. A murder of crows screaming, snare snapping shut in the dark.

You look up from your linguine to ask some vacuous question. My mouth opens like an equator, water filling the room. This reflex is automatic, nothing you can do. It is this water that kills us, the inevitable submersion. Water holding us conscious, unconscious. Unseen currents have killed so many lovers, heads tilted, mouths open.

The marriage didn't end. It simply dissolved as soap in water. I left you sadly, but for other reasons. You must have wanted me around, though, considering everywhere I was. I am piecemeal. I am a treasure map: "Find me."

You want me to act like we've never kissed.
You want to forget, pretend we've never met.
And I've tried, I've tried. You walk by, and I fall
to pieces. Each time I go out with someone
new, you walk by and
            I fall

                  to pie

                        ces

      Y   .
      ou

                  wa

                        lk by, an

      d I fall to
      piec
      es

October, the leaves murdered. A scrap of grace bangs around in the back seat. The light falters. We dream against each other, eyes ravenous, fur in our mouths. Driving north believing in nothing. Each raccoon corpse a talisman. Each blasted road, our own. Here, I love you like sorrow sucking us down salt-deep. A frail cell multiplying in the dark.

Turn, look at me, body curled towards the empty side of the bed. I am a small sulphuric whisper against the wall, swish of tires, wet asphalt. I am a fishing lure, knife against a chopping block. My body double is shadow. I pour from your ears.

You have made me into air; I'm everywhere you look. My limbs ghost the hallways of our apartment; cut the dark corridors, fill them with light.

Imagine it is early. On Dovercourt, the men have retreated, finally back from whence they came. Piss-stained alleys mute and desolate. A woman scurries out from behind the onion-domed church, picks through dumpsters lined against the curb. Rupturing the deaf sleep of the city. Light rises from the streets, fume-like, half-afraid.

"Oh yes," he told the cop. He was sure it was a torso in the garbage bag; layers of flesh raw and carved up, sliced clean through like a bloated Christmas turkey. Slur of semen, spatter of blood lapped up by Lake Ontario. Belly button peeking out like an inanimate third eye. Please come pick it up. It would

have been hard to tell
the sex, except for that scar.
Sexual organs removed
long before she
misplaced
her other
parts.

Eventually, you will decipher where you are. Bags still packed. Lilacs sweating perfume on the lawn. The woman in apartment four delivers her weekly sermon on original sin to anyone who will listen.

On the street someone is screaming. You push through the day, its difficult topography.

Your mutinous language isn't welcome here.
This is not a threat, simply a reminder. In this
pond anyway, you are a fish I eat.

They found me on Remembrance Day in shopping carts and duffel bags. Hands missing. You'd been carrying them around for days. The lawyers said when you killed me you were killing your own conscience. I don't believe that. I know all about how you remember. My hands used to run over objects, a poppy against a shock of white.

Dead sea of marbled green. Flank of earth dug up, filled in. I stretch far into the shadows of the Don Valley. I call from the autumnal dusk, past the screens flickering pornography, rain-soaked garbage. The eternal rumbling of transit.

The viaduct makes makeshift metal crosses against purple skies. Do not look for me standing near the Distress Centre, strategically placed. "Let go." Lake Ontario trembles with light. Do not look for me. I sleep with all drowned things now, the bones of sailors, all those missing children.

The Department of Sanitation scours the city. In the distance, you hear the street-cleaning machine chugging around the corner. Paroxysm of wheels convulsing against pavement. There isn't much time. Soon you will have to get up, make coffee. The underwater light of the television will dissipate into air. You grow heavier as you listen.

Up for hours, you've been listening to nothing. It didn't get you anywhere but here.

You know how I feel about longing. It holds fast, makes you ugly. Wind bruises your lips, desire, the slick pain. You want it anyway, the blind ecstasy of possibility spread-eagle before you. Your face fluoresces under streetlamps. It's always like this: landscape muted, my picture without a face.

We spent three days together. My body shipwrecked, entombed in white porcelain. You asked questions. I didn't answer. You kept me here so I would keep quiet. I drowned over and over in the grouted silence, bloating with indignity and implacable love.

In the meantime, I had become beautiful. I had grown scales and a black, liquid eye. You couldn't see past it, or didn't want to. You cried and went into the kitchen, shuffling through the top drawer for something.

There is meat in the dumpster. You can't pretend it's a mannequin, what with the chipped nail polish, that smell. You could hope she popped ball-socket to ball-socket back into place. Where would it get you? There is still the Avon bracelet, the blood.

The city doesn't pay you enough. For years, you will dream of torsos in tutus. Scissors marching into oblivion. The city couldn't pay you enough. At night, you remove your uniform, fall into bed. You've learned, at least, to sleep.

In the dark, the city looks cleaner. There is a blush about it that makes me unafraid. Landscape unflinching, aurora of artificial light. Around us, a fury of insects, public restrooms, picnic tables, the millpond asleep. Wooden carcasses of swans afloat on its surface.

The light kicks up. For a moment there are cries, the awkward fumbling of animals or teenagers in the bush. Layer after layer of feathers, my hands smelling of balsam. I am risen from your body full of smoke, hundreds of feline-sized rats look up from their midnight feasts. The lake refracts a haze of fuchsia, desire, the black root.

You insist on survival, each kit cramped. Nine tea bags, iodine, elastic bandages. I follow behind. Pocket full of bread crumbs just in case.

We pull over. The sign says FRESH DEW WORMS AND ICE CREAM. The sky gives away nothing. Something is eating you alive – digging through the curvature of your muscle, thin filaments of bone. Small minnows, sharp as Ginsu knives, cut the dark corridors, the echolocation of despair. You turn to me, face full of questions.

"You had a map. You've always had a map."

Suddenly, it is cold. The moon arrives, heaves her swollen belly. I never expected the slight indifference, ice in our hair. What is it you want to say? Say it. "I have never loved you properly, or tried to."

When they come to your house, you'll have to let them in. They'll want to look in your freezer. Making jokes will only make you look heartless, "Well, geez, Officer, if I wanted to kill my wife I woulda used my hands!"

Just show them your power tools and keep quiet. This is murder we're talking about here. You, too, will be a suspect.

I knew what you were doing. Your breath, a purple nimbus, unfettered, reaching across the lake, hooking a thin line of history. The worm coiling and uncoiling, a small fugitive in your hand. You knew something about desire. The way it moves, and how to hold it.

The shopping cart could teach you a thing or two about grief. There is something to be said for how it holds things, what it chooses to let go. Today, you are all about business. What the street sees is anybody's garbage. A tin can, rotting marrow.

In the city, rain drones against the pavement. The streetlights keep burning.

You circle the tree, gesticulating wildly, swilling your Tanqueray, eating year-old popcorn strings. Later, while you are asleep, I will get up and fix everything. Re-align the dollar store lights, spread out the matted tinsel.

For now you smile at the camera as if you really are something. You always thought everything you made was beautiful.

You pull me from the water, glittering and stupid. I have nothing profound to tell you. I speak my own gurgling discourse; a language you cannot understand. Now there is a hook in my lip. I know what you are going to do. I am not afraid of your rogue taxidermy. I know you will make my eyes into glass, add teeth that never bite down.

Things slip by – your body divining for silence. As you wake, the light transcends your fingers; a thin strip of moon passes between them. Tomorrow, you will sign the Christmas cards without me; ink our names indelibly together. What else can be done.

Around us, the people drink booze, look happy. I stare at your face. Your chin is not how I remember it. At twelve, the ball drops. Slow motion confetti quivering into stars. There is no photograph of this. How we kissed at midnight without fireworks or resolution.

I am forgetting your face – anger spreading across it like a dark alphabet. I remember only your body before me. Its solar eclipse. A flash of minnows exploding into night.

Acknowledgements

Some of the poems included in *Exploding into Night* previously appeared in *The Antigonish Review, dANDelion*, and *subTERRAIN*. A selection of the poems was awarded First Place in the 2009 Elora Writers' Festival Poetry Contest. A special thanks to Elana Wolff, my editor, and to Antonio D'Alfonso of Guernica Editions, for their faith in this book. For their love and support I would like to thank my family, Lucy and Neil Pool, Christina and James Bartley, Greg and Jennifer Pool, Elizabeth and Joe Vanderbent , and Jim Johnstone. Also thanks to all those who contributed a discerning eye, or a good kick in the butt where applicable: Dionne Brand, Laura Lush, Connie and Leon Rooke, and the faculty and students of the Guelph MFA program. At the University of Toronto: Camilla Gibb, Djanet Sears, George Elliott Clarke, George Fetherling and Magdalene Redekop. Also: Ken Gass and the staff of Factory Theatre, Pia Kleber and The University College Drama Program, Bridget MacIntosh and the Fringe of Toronto Festival, Jill Frappier, Jack Blum and Sharon Corder, Lindsey Clarke, Sam Cheuk, Leah Jane Esau, Sheniz Janmohamed, Blair Prentice, Shelagh Rowan-Legg, Taylor Graham, Glenn James, Wayne Strongman and the folks at Tapestry New Opera Works, and, as always, Erin, Ontario.

Printed in November 2009
at Gauvin Press,
Gatineau, Québec

The
Psychology
of Sales

A Personal Guide for Success

Matt Wells

TABLE OF CONTENTS

This booklet guide is a tool to help you make positive changes to the way you approach sales and other aspects of your life. It can be a stand alone product but is best used when combined with the Psychology of Selling DVD. To order the DVD or to download a copy go to: <u>a-fect.com</u> or <u>vimeo.com/afect</u>.

Enjoy this guide, the DVD or both and do everything in your power to listen closely or read and apply to make the changes necessary to be extremely successful in today's markets.

*"Education is the most powerful weapon
which you can use to change the world"*
Nelson Mandela

Most all sales people have been taught
to be persuasive in their approach to
sales. Sales training has been done on
a "silver platter" basis - tell me what to
do and when. This practice of training
eliminates the value of individual
personalities. WE have been taught
procedurally what to do but most people
do not know *WHY* they do what they do.

This seminar is about understanding
where the sales industry is today in our
country (and others) and being able to
make the changes necessary to cope
with how business owners purchase. If
we understand how our clients naturally
purchase, then it is much easier to make
a sale.

Chapter 1

Why Change

The idea of change scares many people. When the changes help to elicit more success, then change becomes easy. The first part of changing is understanding WHY we need to change - even more so than HOW. The sales strategies of the past have been based on convincing the client they have a need for your product. We have done this by:

Completely focussing on our product.

Tell the client what is important about your product.

Promote the features and benefits of the products.

Use several different closing techniques to GET them to buy.

Use several different objection handling techniques when they say "No".

We know this is true just by listening to the common conversations sales people have when they talk about

"getting a client".

This produces a sense of a battle that one person wins and the other loses. Not sure why we want to think of our clients as
"losing"

when they buy our product. Proving value has been a big issue. Tell and show the client the value of your product. Pound on your chest to prove to the client you have what they need.

VALUE

In future seminars, we will discuss at length that the value you are proving is your own, not the client's. We need to find the client's value issues and work with them to see how the product fits their business.

WHOSE SAVVY???

There is a new breed of owner in our midsts in America. The owners of today have different philosophies than they did 15 or 20 years ago. Their attitude toward sales have changed. They are more sales savvy than they have ever been in history. The business owners of today have read the books, watched the DVD's, downloaded seminars and attended seminars on sales in order to enhance the sales in their own business. These are the same training seminars that sales people attend. Therefore, they know the plays. If a sales person and client learned the same information about sales and the client is approached in that manner, then the client can call the shots because they recognize the strategy.

Business owners do not want to be sold in today's world,

they want to know that a product is right for their business and can visualize how the product will work within the confines of their business.

Change number one

Understand that you must find out all you can about the client, what they are doing currently in their business, why they perform that way, where they are taking the business and why. This way, you can see how your product will fit their normal way of doing business.

"Find out how your product fits the client rather than trying to make the client fit your product."

PRACTICE:
Write down five questions that you could ask that will give you better insight to the way an owner is doing business.

1.

2.

3.

4.

5.

"The world as we have created it is a process of our thinking. It cannot be changed without changing our thinking." Albert Einstein

Chapter #2

Oh, It's All About Me!

Several publications in the U.S. (i.e. Time, Newsweek) have done articles on the extreme narcissism in our country.

"It is all about me"

seems to be the battle cry in American business. It's not hard to look around and see narcissism every where you go. Because of this,

change number two

must occur. This change is about how you approach your customers. In the last eight years or so, business owners have become less concerned about what YOU think is important with your product and become more concerned with their own product(s). Whether you like narcissism or not, it is here and we must deal with it.

(training + change + passion = success)

Dealing with this new state of mind means we must be more concerned about the client than we are of selling our product. Therefore, make sure that everything you do and say is

100%

about the client. In doing so, the client will tell you all the different ways you need to approach them in order for them to purchase from you.

Listening is the ultimate skill to master

We all think we are good listeners, but that is just not true. We hear the words but do not find the meaning through listening. We get more concerned with hearing buying signals than listening to the subtle ways they tell us how to sell them. Get rid of your sales agenda in your mind and keep a focus on asking questions that deal with the client's opinion.

"To SUCCEED in business, you must be RELEVANT - making CHANGES keeps you RELEVANT!"
        Matt Wells

If you don't like change, you will certainly hate extinction!

By:KW Photography

LISTEN:

Questions are the key, but listening between the lines is the skill

Stay away from leading questions that have a sales content to them. Ask the client about their business, how they made it so successful and ask them why?. The answer to the question why will create a vision for you as to how your product will fit their business. Why is the least asked question but will reveal the most important information. There are several ways to ask the question why without using the word why. Ask questions like

**"so why is that so important...?"
or
"how did you know to do ....?".**

Speak the client's language by relating questions and analogies that deal with a portion of their business. This will help them to see that you understand and have an interest in their business. Get in tune with their business rather than your agenda on making a sale and, please, keep things in perspective. The questions do not have to deal with making the sale or leading the client to a sale but should be about their

opinion.

This is a hard change since most sales people have been taught to guide the client to the sale. Let the client guide you to the sale so you know how your products fits them.

PRACTICE:
Write down two reasons to keep the focus entirely on the client's business.

1.

2.

"In our ever changing world, understanding the psychology of this new sales world is the most crucial step to success."
Matt Wells

Chapter #3

Are You Up For It?

There is an old saying that is very true:

"If you continue to do what you have always done and expect different results, then you are insane."

Clients call A-Fect Sales and Management Training when they finally come to a realization that what they have done and what they are doing is not eliciting the sought after results. They need CHANGE.

This is change number three.

Do you have the ability or the guts to go inside your business (or yourself) and decide that nothing will change without making a change? Suck up the pride and have the guts to ask for help. This is an **attitude** that breeds success.

Attitude is one of the most important issues in sales.

If we take on the humility to be willing to learn new and exciting things, then we become more excited and successful. Humility with clients is also extremely important. The business owners today want a real person sitting in front of them, not a sales person with a distinct and recognizable strategy. Listen closely to this part of the DVD when talking about humility, having an aura of calmness and confidence (without cockiness) and control your voice content. Stop selling so hard and start putting that same effort into asking questions and listening intently.

"Just one week after the training (from A-Fect) one of our reps sales were up 400%".
       Nex-Tech

PRACTICE:

Do a role play with a colleague and listen for strategy, sales jargon, a push for the product, and listen to see what agenda they are on. Take note on how much of the role play was about the client, the client's desires in business and see if the they asked questions to discover the client's value of the product(s).

Test yourself on your listening skills to see how much you can discover about your colleague's selling technique.

"Success in sales demands a shift in sales strategies, direction and philosophy".
                    Matt Wells

Chapter #4

You Tawkin' to Me?

To help you in making changes to
your selling program, let's take a look at
the different types of personalities in the
work force today. The age brackets
described below are all generalities as
are the depiction of their personalities.
But these generalities will help you to
understand who you are dealing with
and the changes you can make to get in
tune with your clients.

Matures
Ages 65 and above. These people have
been there and done that. Therefore,
they are in a more nurturing and
mentoring state than others. They want
to help people they work with be
successful. The Matures' self worth is
based on giving to others. The more
they can give of themselves, the better
they feel. Their social life is within the
confines of work or in small groups
outside work for playing games.
Approaching the mature business owner
is best done in light of wanting their

input or helping you gain some of their wisdom.

PRACTICE:
Write a question that may stimulate a conversation with a Mature.

Did you start one of your responses with the question "I would really like your input on…..?", or "Could you help me with….?", "I would really like your help in understanding…?".

Baby Boomers

Ages 45 - 65. These are the workhorses
of the business world. They are very
driven when it comes to work. They like
to climb the corporate ladder in order to
gain recognition and and are proud of
promotions. Their idea is that the higher
they are on the chain, the more money
they make so the better they are able to
care for their family. They are willing to,
and often do, spend a lot of time at work
or travel extensively for work. Their self
worth is in line with their status at work.
Many Baby Boomers will have what is
known as an "I love me wall" in their
office where they hang diplomas and
achievements. Most often their social
life is also based on work. They do not
have many friends outside of work but
the ones they have are very close.
Working a 14 hour day is not uncommon
for a Boomer. Approaching a Boomer
requires being a real person. They want
to create a relationship with you but it
can only be done if they respect you as
a real person. You don't have to relate
anything about your personal life with
them but approach them with honest

respect and create a relationship based on business.

PRACTICE:
Write down all the qualities of a Baby Boomer that you know and see how many fit the profile. Then ask them how they like to be approached by sales people and why.

"And that is how change happens. One gesture. One person. One moment in time."
            Libba Bray

Generation X

Ages 30 - 45. The Gen X wants to work hard at work as long as it is in the confines of the set hours of the day (i.e. 8 to 5). They do not like wasting time at work because their self worth is within the family. They will do all they can to make sure adequate and substantial time is spent with the family rather than at work. Their social life revolves around their kids. They like to take part in all activities that their kids are involved with. They will accept promotions as long as there is not a greater requirement for time spent at work and therefore away from the family. When approaching a Gen X business owner, they need to feel you are sincere about THEIR business and time. Examine what they do in their company and see if your product can help them get more done in a shorter period of time.

PRACTICE:
Consult with a colleague that is a Gen X. Write down approaches that would get appointments according to your colleague.

"Everyone thinks of changing the world, but no one thinks of changing himself."
    Leo Tolstoy

Generation Y

Ages 30 and under. This generation wants the CEO job upon being hired. They are very technically minded and like to use technology to make life easier at work. They are not as socially developed as the other generations but do like to work in groups. Working alone is not something a Gen Y will often do. Their self worth is more aligned with social media - i.e. how many friends they have on Facebook or how many texts they received in a day. Approach them with the idea that you will be working together and the more technically minded the approach, the better.

PRACTICE:

Find all the technical items you can about your product and find ways it helps speed up the work day.

There was a study done recently that depicts the generations to a "T". This may help in understanding your approach.

A company decided to give out hourly passes to people who have gone above and beyond the call of duty. These passes could be used at any time. They could take an hour at the beginning of work, get out an hour early or use several at a time for half or full days off. When asked how they were used by the different generations, this is how it went:

Matures - Gave their passes away to colleagues who really needed the time off.

Baby Boomers - Collected the passes and hung them on their wall to show people the great work they have done.

Gen X - Would use them to get off an hour early to go to their kids soccer game.

Gen Y - Would take them immediately after receiving them and run to their car and text for an hour.

PRACTICE:
Write down a series of questions based on the information above that would help you engage with the different genders.

Matures:

Baby Boomers:

Generation X:

Generation Y:

"Don't be fooled by training material that is 10 or more years old - old is old."

Chapter #5

Three Excellent Words

At the beginning of this DVD we talked about understanding how people buy.

This is the most relevant thought in sales today.

If we understand how people naturally buy, then it is relatively easy to fit your products within their scope of business. The best part is that most everyone purchases the same way. There are three words to keep in mind that will help you with understanding how people purchase.

Purpose. The word purpose is huge in sales. We often see sales people that try to sell a product to a client or try to increase a current client's purchase without any purpose for the client. Most sales people have a purpose in mind when they approach a client but that is their own purpose not the purpose of the client. Get in tune with your client to make sure that when you present your product that it has a definitive purpose for the client.

Appropriate. Finding out how and why your client does business will allow you to find ways that make your product appropriate for your client. Make it fit their way of doing business, their culture of their company and make sure it is appropriate for where the client is taking their business.

Expectation. Your product must meet or exceed your client's expectation. The only way to find the expectation is by asking. Find the expectation and produce a product that can meet it.Most all people purchase this way. We buy a certain car because it serves a purpose for us, is appropriate for what we want to accomplish and in some way meets or exceeds our expectation. We all do this at the grocery store. The food we buy is for a purpose, is appropriate for what we want to accomplish with the food and the products meet or exceed our expectation.

Live by these three words

In future DVDs and booklets we will discuss other uses of these three words that are extremely dynamic.

PRACTICE:

Write down, in your words, why you think the three words described previously are important and how you will use them in approaching clients.

"Here's to the crazy ones. The misfits. The rebels. The troublemakers. The round pegs in the square holes. The ones who see things differently. They're not fond of rules. And they have no respect for the status quo. You can quote them, disagree with them, glorify or vilify them. About the only thing you can't do is ignore them. Because they change things. They push the human race forward. And while some may see them as the crazy ones, we see genius. Because the people who are crazy enough to think they can change the world, are the ones who do."
  Apple Inc.

FINAL THOUGHTS FOR TODAY

Most sales people want their productivity to go up, their income to increase and their job to be less stressful. This DVD will help you in starting this shift in sales. Nothing can be done without you making a conscious decision to change. A great opportunity is staring you right in the face -RIGHT NOW!! You have the ability to change at this time, at this moment. The opportunity is now - not tomorrow, not next week, not when you have thought it through, not when you feel like it. etc. Take advantage of it now.

Your contract is on the next page.

"Change Doesn't happen later, change happens now." Matt Wells

My Personal Contract for Change

This is a contract to maximize my ability and productivity. By adhering to and signing this contract, I am making a conscious decision to change in whatever way is necessary and possible to drive myself to the levels of success I determine.

This is binding agreement with myself and if the contract is broken, my penalty will be long lasting unnecessary struggles.

Therefore, I hereby choose to make changes today in order to improve my life today.

I will put my initials next to each item that I am serious about after viewing this life-changing program.

___I am 100% willing to make change
___I will put maximum effort into making positive changes

___I agree that my efforts will be the determining factors of my results
___I will trust that the information given will help lead me out of my comfort zone
___I will share information with others to help them be stronger

I am signing out of free will to be the best I can be at all times.

_____   _____

your signature   date

_____   _____

witness signature   date

A-Fect is also available to give opportunities for success to sales people and managers with personal visits to your place of business. These seminars have proven to make dramatic changes in the productivity of sales and increased incomes. With personal visits, your specific situations and concerns can be directly addressed with several solutions to help you and sales teams make the changes to be more successful. Call or go online and ask about a program that will be specifically designed for you.

To order or download a copy of the DVD go to a-fect.com or vimeo.com/afect.

We have had Matt Wells at Mueller Publishing three times. We were impressed with how well he understood the YP markets. He was able to show us an effective way of selling that WORKED!! Times have changed, and Matt is ahead of the game with sales training. we would definitely recommend him and look forward to having him back at our company.

THANK YOU MATT for boosting our sales year after year. You have been a big influence on our doublo digit increases.

Mueller Publishing

ABOUT A-FECT

A-Fect was started in 2001 as a company to deliver a different style of sales idea to the selling community. Over the course of the last 13 years, A-Fect has helped hundreds of sales organizations and individual sales people all over the United States and Canada.

The uniqueness of the information is the strategy for learning that A-Fect developed over the years that no other training company has. The learning curve for people that attend A-Fect seminars is very high and retention is fantastic.

The best part, is that individuals can continue to teach themselves after the training. Therefore, A-Fect has the number one sales concept in the United States and Canada for helping sales people and organizations grow beyond their expectations.

Visit A-Fect.com to learn more.

Matt T. Wells

First of all, **CONGRATULATIONS** on taking the first step to improving yourself. As you improve, everything around you gets better. Colleagues and clients respond more positively to you. Friends and family see you in a brighter light.

The only way to do this is to change.

As a former teacher I hope you gained value from the information provided in this DVD. As a former Commander in the U.S. Air Force, I employ you to put the strategies to work for yourself and see what happens. There is only one way to improve on the information given here today - schedule an on site training session where we can get down to the targeted items that you know will help you most. Take care and I look forward to meeting you in person in the near future

"He who rejects change is the architect of decay. The only human institution which rejects progress is the cemetery."
~Harold Wilson

By:KW Photography

Printed in Great Britain
by Amazon